# THE HEART OF A MEDIC

By: Phillip Gray

Cover illustrated by:
William Smoot

Copyright © 2012 Phillip Gray, all rights reserved

This book and all works comprised in it are copyright and no part of it may in any form or by any means (including without limitation, electronic, mechanical, micro-copying, photocopying, recording, scanning or otherwise) be modified, reproduced, stored in a retrieval system, published, broadcast, distributed or transmitted without prior written permission of the Author, Phillip Gray. No express or implied license to use any part of these works is granted to any person without the express prior written consent of Phillip Gray and any implied license to use any part of these works is expressly forbidden.

Cover Art Copyright © 2012 William Smoot, all rights reserved

The Cover Art of this book is copyright of William Smoot and may not be used in any form or by any means (including without limitation, electronic, mechanical, micro-copying, photocopying, recording, scanning or otherwise) be modified, reproduced, stored in a retrieval system, published, broadcast, distributed or transmitted without prior written permission of William Smoot or his authorized agent and any implied license to use any part of these works is expressly forbidden.

## Dedication:

This book is dedicated to my wife, Leora, who has patiently allowed me to read to her every poem included here. Without her dedication and loving inspiration, this work would not have been published.

Thanks honey, I love you always.

Phillip Gray

*To Kailey*

# Table of Contents

- WHAT IS THIS NATION? ..... 1
- MEDIC ..... 2
- ARMY ..... 3
- NAVY ..... 4
- MARINES ..... 5
- COAST GUARD ..... 6
- AIR FORCE ..... 7
- SENT TO WAR ..... 8
- MOMS OF WAR ..... 9
- DADS OF WAR ..... 10
- WIVES OF WAR ..... 11
- CHILDREN OF WAR ..... 12
- WAR ..... 13
- SERVING MY COUNTRY ..... 14
- HEROES ..... 15
- I KNEW A YOUNG BOY ..... 16
- THANKSGIVING DAY ..... 17
- CHRISTMAS DAY ..... 18
- INDEPENDENCE DAY ..... 19
- HE CAME FROM NOWHERE ..... 20
- A LIFE WITHOUT LOVE ..... 21
- MARRIED ..... 21

## Table of Contents

| | |
|---|---|
| THE MEANING OF LIFE | 22 |
| LIFE'S WORTH | 23 |
| POEMS | 24 |
| FREEDOM | 25 |
| MY WIFE | 26 |
| MY SON | 27 |
| MY DAUGHTER | 28 |
| STARS | 29 |
| LOVE CAN BE PAIN | 30 |
| BABBLING BROOK | 31 |
| THE SPIRIT OF MAN | 32 |
| THE CLOWN | 33 |
| LIFE IS A PLAY | 34 |
| FATE OF MAN | 35 |
| MEN AND WOMEN | 36 |
| MIRACLES | 37 |
| TEACHERS | 38 |
| A MAN | 39 |
| FRIENDSHIP | 40 |
| MY DOGGIE | 41 |
| A SOLDIER'S TOAST | 42 |
| THAT WAS MY MOTHER | 43 |

# What is this Nation?

What is this Nation, that we call home,
Is it a song we sing so loud and clear,
Is it a flag we hail flying proud and free,
Or is it the hearts of its people, free from fear?

This Nation, my home these many years,
Is more than the people in power,
That led this Nation through times good and bad,
Oh no, my man, this Nation over this does tower.

This Nation, the greatest history has seen,
Is more than a flag that flies proud and true,
A flag we have honored and fought for,
Oh no, my friend, it is more than red, white, and blue.

This Nation, teaming from shore to shore,
Is more than the song we proudly sing,
A song penned by a patriot so long ago,
Oh no, dear reader, more loudly it does ring.

This Nation, with people so diverse,
Is more than the sum of all its' parts,
For all its' people come from distant shores,
Oh no, my people, it's true meaning is in our hearts.

So what is this Nation we call home,
It is for all the people living here to say,
For this nation is one people united,
Oh yes, dear world, it is the great and proud USA.

# Medic

A man is down, the call goes out,
"MEDIC", the cry ripples like a wave,
Response is quick, for without a doubt,
Our skills are needed, a life to save.

These soldiers are our friends,
Closer than brothers are we,
Now, upon us their life depends,
We treat their wounds on bended knee.

We treat the body, the soul, the mind,
With open heart, trained eye and hand,
With diligence their wounds we bind,
We do our best to save as many as we can.

We fight a powerful enemy we cannot see,
For he stalks our friends by night and day,
Death himself is a Medics only real enemy,
Between death and friends is where we stay.

We fight our enemy not with knife or gun,
But with faith, and hope, and skill,
We never give up until the battle is done,
Fighting to preserve life, not to kill.

To the battles we lose, we can only say,
To our brothers, we did give our all,
For those we have lost along the way,
Your memories will never fail, or fall.

# Army

Over hill, over dale,
With this, we never fail,
For we are soldiers fighting for what is right.
Desert, jungles, or snow,
Ever doing what we know,
Keeping our country's freedom always in sight.

Fighting soldiers that never quit,
Quick and hard is how we hit,
Going forward for the free and the brave.
What we desire is peace,
Our desire will never cease,
But fight if we must, our freedom to save.

The Army is what we are,
Leaving home and going afar,
Always praying for peace wherever we go.
Standing tall and looking good,
Standing for freedom as we should,
For our country we stand against every foe.

Many soldiers have been lost,
Paying the ultimate horrible cost,
To insure that our country will never fall.
The souls of these women and men,
The faces that we'll never see again,
Their names are printed upon our heart's wall.

Come join our parade,
As we wade into the fray,
Standing watch over our country so vast and free.
From the start we have stood,
Standing for freedom, as all men should,
Fighting for freedom for all the world to see.

# Navy

We sail the seas and watch the sky,
Fighting so freedom will never die,
We sail for freedom across the oceans and seas.
Facing the enemy on sea and land,
We keep freedom close at hand,
Fighting sailors is what we will always be.

From harm we keep the seven seas,
Fighting to keep our country free,
Fighting for freedom from our countries start.
Our ships are big and fast,
Built tough, built to last,
With our families we know we must daily part.

The Navy is what we do and are,
From home we sail very far,
Keeping the world safe for freedoms call.
From the ships, our planes we fly,
Preserving freedom from the sky,
We valiantly sail to each and every port of call.

To Davy's Locker some have gone,
But their memories will live on,
They died to keep our country safe and free.
We honor those that we have lost,
For freedom they paid the cost,
These sailors do rest beneath the sky and the sea.

Come and watch as we sail,
On the seas we will prevail,
Preserving our freedom on air, land, and sea.
As sailors we will never fail,
Keeping watch under a sail,
We are the Navy; we sail for the brave and the free.

## Marines

Last to leave, first to go in,
This how we fight and win,
Leatherneck is what we are sometimes called.
We fight and never quit,
We keep ourselves trim and fit,
Never allowing freedom to be stopped or stalled.

"Semper Fi", is what we say,
Keeping the peace day by day,
We walk the walls, tyranny and freedom we divide.
We stand until the enemy does run,
Fighting at night and in the sun,
We are standing tall with respect, honor, and pride.

With honor we always stand,
Keeping faith close at hand,
As Marines, we protect the small and weak.
With our brothers we stand tall,
So that freedom will never fall,
But still, peace is what we will always seek.

For freedom is where we stand,
We lend the weak a helping hand,
And keep our honor standing straight and tall.
We stand and fight as good men should,
We never quit as weaker men could,
Keeping the watch so freedom can never fall.

To the few we have lost,
For freedom paying the cost,
Their sacrifice for freedom will never fail or fall.
The ultimate price, they did pay,
Fighting for freedom day by day,
Leaving this life with pride and honor, standing tall

## Coast Guard

Our country's coast we guard,
And this job can be hard,
We are the Coast Guard, standing vigil day and night.
We sail and watch over the nearest seas,
Against our enemy's we never freeze,
For our country, we serve and if need be, we fight.

We feel our service is the best,
For each of us has passed the test,
As patriots, we sail, protect, rescue, and serve.
From many services is how we grew,
Always serving red, white, and blue,
We sail with pride and never lose our nerve.

Rescuing people every day,
Helping them find their way,
Safely back home to family and friends.
On the seas you can see us sail,
Calm seas when storms do wail,
For this is our sacred task that never ends.

Sisters and brothers we have lost to the sea,
Insuring that others can be safe and free,
To our comrades we give our sacred devotion
Their lives will never be lost in vain,
To their duty and honor they did never wane,
We commit their soul and memory to the ocean.

So come and join if you dare,
To show the world you care,
To protect our freedom here at home.
Stand with us off our shores,
Keeping open freedom's doors,
Defending freedom from upon the foam.

## Air Force

Look in the sky, you will see
Where we fight for the free,
Sailing the skies to watch over our land.
Our people are the best,
And have risen to the test,
Flying for the freedom is where we live and stand.

We answered to the Airmen's call,
We will never falter, fail, or fall,
Flying for freedom, keeping a watchful eye.
We serve on land and in the sky,
For freedom, if we must, we will die,
Keeping our country safe, watching from on high.

Few will ever be able to claim,
The Airman's call to fame,
For we proudly serve the brave and the free.
We come from each and every state,
Standing for freedom true and straight,
So look into the sky, that is where we will be.

Some flyers have paid the cost,
So our freedom will not be lost,
We honor these heroes for freedom, they gave their all.
Now they rest beneath the sky,
Their memories will never die,
To protect our freedom, answering our nation's call.

Come out and watch us fly,
As we serve in the sky,
For we are Airmen, proud, brave, and true.
Our country is what we serve,
From our duty we'll never swerve,
We are the ones who proudly wear the blue

## Sent To War

We send our sons to war,
It seems more and more,
And we pray they come home alive and well.
They go to foreign lands,
They are in God's hands,
We wait, watch, and pray, 'cause we know war is hell.

The used to go by trains,
Now they go by planes,
But that is the only change, for war is always the same.
They still leave loved ones behind,
A strange new world they will find,
And shortly they learn they will never be the same.

Many friends they will lose,
But they will continue to choose,
To fight for freedom on every land and shore.
Many battles they will fight,
For they know this is right,
Praying someday to put an end to war.

When home again they come,
With souls that are numb,
And with visions of death they left behind.
Welcome them with open arms,
Hugs, kisses, and all our charms,
For they are heroes, none better will you find.

## Moms of War

Her baby goes off to fight,
She knows this is right,
But her heart is broken, torn, and sad.
She raised her child to love,
Not a hawk, but a dove,
And now turns for comfort to his dad.

She awaits her baby's return,
Many tears she will burn,
For the baby from her womb is off to war.
She cries herself to sleep,
Fond memories she will keep,
Until her baby again walks through her door.

Quite often we forget,
To our shame and regret,
Our moms fight our wars as well.
They fight from their homes,
While their little baby roams,
They too have to live a life of hell.

To these forgotten heroes,
With rewards that equal zero,
We owe a debt we cannot begin to pay.
I salute the Moms of War,
Heroes they are, and more,
For their love and devotion grows day after day.

# Dads of War

He offers his loving hand,
His little boy is now a man,
With pride he sees him straight and tall.
Then he looks at his wife,
In her eyes, he sees her strife,
Their son is answering his country's call.

His cute little boy is what he'll see,
Playing so happy and carefree,
To a big strong man he watched him grow.
In his uniform he seems so big,
In his heart, he'll have to dig,
To find the strength to let his little boy go.

His loving wife he'll try to console,
He knows in her heart there is a hole,
As they watch their little boy walk away.
While he is gone, he will try,
To wipe the tear from her eye,
Every day for his safe return they will pray.

Come home alive is all he could say,
I've tried to teach you along the way,
This one thing is all I am asking in return.
And so he watches his little boy,
With pride, but without the joy,
For in his heart pain and anguish will burn.

Dads of War you are the very best,
You taught your son to pass the test.
Because of you, a good and upright man he'll be.
For freedom, your son will fight,
In your heart, you know it is right,
Your son will help to keep our nation free.

## Wives of War

To her husband she says goodbye,
In her heart, silently she will cry,
She doesn't know if home again he'll come.
Alone tonight in bed she'll sleep,
In her heart, hope she will keep,
Until he returns, her heart is sad and numb.

Her country he serves with pride,
Her anguish she finds hard to hide,
Awards to his chest she knows they'll pin.
With her should be her man,
She will always be his biggest fan.
She longs to hold him in her arms once again.

Their children safe she'll keep,
Not letting them watch her weep,
For her family she'll pretend to be strong.
But, alone in her room at night,
She cannot hide her dreadful plight,
Each and every night seems forever to go on.

But when the day does dawn,
She will continue to go on,
Keeping the home fires burning so bright.
For his safe return she will long,
But till that day she'll stay strong,
Her tears and anguish she'll keep out of site.

When the day does finally come,
Into his loving arms she'll run,
Tears of loving joy will stain her face.
Her loving man again is home,
She prays again he'll never roam,
By her side he'll take his rightful place.

# Children of War

His daddy is off to fight,
His heart feels so tight,
Will his daddy come home to him again?
He really wants to cry,
He doesn't understand why,
His daddy has to go and fight the bad men.

Mommy is sad he knows,
In her loving face it shows,
She tries so very hard to hide the pain.
Her little man he'll try to be,
Her pain he'll try not to see,
But his world seems to have gone insane.

While his daddy is gone,
He'll try to do no wrong,
To his daddy he promised not to be bad.
He said he'd be his best,
Trying not to be a pest,
For he knows his mommy's heart is sad.

He'll keep a faithful watch,
Waiting for his daddy to march,
Back home to his loving little boy again.
Home his daddy should be,
He wants his daddy to see,
How high his big boy held his little chin.

To these children I can only say,
Your daddy is going far away,
Around the world, children he will protect.
See the hero that is your dad,
Try your best not to be sad,
Your daddy deserves all your love and respect.

## War

I ask myself what good is a war,
Can you tell me what can it be for,
But to protect the weak, the innocent, the small.
If it is war we must fight,
Let it be for what is right,
'Cause freedom must be preserved for all.

We do fight only if we must,
For in God we do give our trust,
To bring us back home to those we left behind.
What we really desire is peace,
For this our desire will never cease,
For peace should be the final goal of all mankind.

Fighting to keep freedom alive,
For this goal we always do strive,
For freedom, there is no cost that is too great.
Some think the opposite of war is peace,
But often without war, evil will release,
Slavery and tyranny would be our ultimate fate.

Good men and women will be lost,
For this is the ultimate, deadly cost,
To defend the right of freedom on every shore.
To honor those brave women and men,
We know we must fight until we win,
To insure the light of freedom for ever more.

For peace we will always pray,
Wiping away the clouds of gray,
A world of peace should be our ultimate goal.
But as evil men continue to rise,
All good men must be wise,
Defeating evil and, if need be, paying the toll.

# Serving My Country

My country I wanted to serve,
My resolve did never swerve,
With the Army I decided I needed to be.
As a Medic, lives I could save,
This is what my heart did crave,
Treating the soldiers, keeping my country free.

My training was the best,
I finally passed the test,
A Medic going off to serve with pride.
I wanted to stand and be strong,
I knew this couldn't be wrong,
The fear I felt in my heart, I pushed aside.

The lesson I was to learn,
Death would take its' turn,
Many good men would suffer and die.
For those I lost, I cried,
I knew my best I tried,
But to the heavens silently I ask, why?

A friend then said to me,
The answer can only be,
In war, only two rules always prevail.
Good men are bound to die,
You'll never find a reason why,
If you try to change this, you will fail.

So with this, I did go on,
Fighting dawn till dawn,
Fighting death wherever I happen to be,
With death, I will always fight,
For I know that this is right,
Using my skill to save all those I can see.

# Heroes

Heroes is what they say we are,
From the truth, this is very far,
But ordinary women and men doing a job.
Heroes are buried in the ground,
Their like again will not be found,
For death himself, their lives from us did rob.

Medals on our chest they pin,
Then we go back to do it again,
Just doing our job the way we were taught.
Our friends are standing at our side,
From them, our fear we cannot hide,
Never knowing the why of the plan or plot.

With these good friends we daily live,
Our own lives we would freely give,
To see them homeward bound, safe and free.
We remember each and every face,
In our heart, they have a special place,
Where forever they will live triumphantly.

To these heroes I can only say,
There will never come a day,
When your memory will fall from our mind.
For to us you will always live,
Your last devotion you did give,
Because of you, our courage we did find.

If heroes you really want to see,
Do not look at her, or him, or me,
In heaven is where our heroes are living now.
Honor their memory every day,
And let us all hope and pray,
An end to fallen heroes must be our sacred vow.

## I knew a young boy

I knew a boy that went to war,
That boy was seen never more,
For one night he died and was born anew.
This boy grew old in just one night,
He never gave in to his dreadful fright,
In a few short hours, to manhood he grew.

I wonder who was this young boy,
That war was willing to destroy,
Killing his essence, his heart, his soul.
His innocence he forever lost,
For his country, he paid the cost,
For war always demands the heaviest toll.

In his body, a new man was born,
With a heart and soul forever torn,
Always wondering about the boy he left behind.
About this boy this man would ask,
Hoping someday the boy to unmask,
His hopes and dreams he desperately tried to find.

He would ponder for many years,
About the boy's hopes and fears,
From life, what did this young boy deeply yearn.
What dreams did he hold dear,
To what principles did he adhere,
To this young boy's innocence he wanted to return.

I wish I could know this young boy,
I wish he was here to share his joy,
So life through his eyes all the world could see.
I desperately look for him in every place,
I search in each and every single face,
For the man that took his place in life was me.

# Thanksgiving Day

Thanksgiving is the wonderful day,
For all we have special thanks we give.
Each year it's our unique and special way,
The Pilgrim's beginning we try to relive.

Many holidays throughout the year,
We celebrate with family and friends.
We sing, we laugh, we cherish, we cheer,
Hoping this very special day never ends.

Thanksgiving should be given every day,
So many things we have to be thankful for,
In our hearts, Thanksgiving should never stray,
With thanks living, our Thanksgiving will soar.

Look around you each and every day,
To see how truly happy and blessed you are.
Then list all the blessings you have today,
You'll find that happiness isn't very far.

Always stay thankful so that others can see,
The path to happiness and joy you've found.
The more thankful you are willing to be,
In your heart, more joy and peace will abound.

To all I wish to give this special toast,
That thankful we live each and every day.
Thankful people truly have the very most,
To be thankful for on Thanksgiving Day.

## Christmas Day

Christmas morning is the best,
A day to give and a day to rest,
Never forgetting the birth we celebrate.
We eat a big and wonderful feast,
We carve the best, juiciest beast,
Our family and friends eagerly we await.

Good gifts we give with glee,
We really can't wait to see,
The joy on their faces at the gifts we give.
Packages are opened so very fast,
Before we know, the morn is past,
But the joy in our hearts continues to live.

We look forward all year long,
Looking forward can't be wrong,
For we know Christmas is never very far away.
Opening presents that we are given,
Sometimes like demons we are driven,
To rip and tear the colorful wrappings away.

But let us not forget in our haste,
On whose birth this day is based,
For in our zeal, we sometimes tend to forget.
There is a wonderful reason,
For this wonderful season,
It is the life of whom we all owe the greatest debt.

For in a manger he was born,
A promise to us was sworn,
That his life would make us alive and whole.
He grew into a great, upright man,
He gave us the most wonderful plan,
Showing us life's ultimate and wonderful goal.

# Independence Day

Every year on the fourth of July,
Great colorful fireworks tend to fly,
We watch as the black night sky is brightly lit.
Our mighty flag we proudly raise,
Our forefathers we want to praise,
For independence, they fought and never quit.

On a picnic frequently we go,
On the grill we want to throw,
Hot dogs, hamburgers, and simple fare.
We eat till our bellies full are,
We play the fiddle and guitar,
Loudly singing songs with a patriotic flair.

I think I love this day the most,
For this is the day when we boast,
Of how our independence and freedom we won.
The document they signed long ago,
Helped this beautiful country to grow,
The light of a new, wonderful nation did dawn.

The fireworks that we love to display,
It shows the world we are here to stay,
We want each and every nation to clearly see.
Our country may be younger than most,
This country will always loudly boast,
We are a nation where all the people are free.

Come and join me on July the fourth,
Whether from the south or the north,
A united nation is what we will always be.
Celebrate and have some fun,
Sitting out in the bright sun,
Then in the night the bright fireworks we'll see.

## He Came From Nowhere

He came into my life out of nowhere,
Like the Arthurian Knights of old,
To most, a plain and ordinary man,
But to me, a treasure greater than gold.

He didn't wear a white hat, or ride a mighty horse,
Nor did he slay great dragons with a mighty sword.
But to me, he was the greatest of all the heroes,
Because of his caring, my life and spirit soared.

He didn't wear a bright and colorful costume,
He didn't have a secret cave, as some heroes do.
He just provided a loving and caring home,
As only a real hero is willing and able to do.

He encouraged me to be my very best,
He taught about how to be a real dad.
He loved me, asking nothing in return,
He comforted me when I was down and sad.

My mother is the one he loved the most,
Children not his own he did raise and love.
He gave to us all his strength and wisdom,
As to great men, he stands far above.

Gone is he now, gone to his just reward,
I miss him deeply, more than any can know.
With what he has engraved in my heart and mind,
His life continues within me, living within my soul.

## A Life without Love
(My very first poem, written at the age of 18 in Vietnam)

A life without love,
Is a life short lived,
A life without love,
Is a life God won't forgive.

A life without love,
Is meaningless and sore,
A life without love,
Is Life no more.

## Married

I married a young girl,
So sweet and so fine,
But over the years I found,
She wasn't very kind.

I married a fine lady,
So prim and proper,
But she treated me badly,
And so I had to drop her.

I married a good woman,
That knew how to love a man,
And so now I'm happy,
Now this marriage will stand.

So, when looking for a wife,
Find a friend for all time,
A woman that will love you,
Throughout your lifetime.

# The Meaning of Life

What is the meaning of life,
This is the question I would ask,
This journey I have traveled,
What is the goal of this arduous task?

I have walked life's highways,
I have hiked each path I've found,
But I still have to wonder why,
To what purpose do I abound?

I have helped many people,
In need along life's winding way,
I offer a hand to help them up,
But as to why, I cannot say.

My spirit has soared to the heavens,
And then dashed down to the earth below,
But still the answer eludes me,
To what purpose do I onward go.

Life seems to be a journey onward,
But I cannot see the ending goal,
I seem to wander aimlessly,
With no map or guide the way to show.

And so I continue onward, my friend,
Each step leading to an unknown shoal,
But still the question remains within me,
The meaning of life, I still do not know.

Perhaps I am not meant to have the answer,
And must wait for that eventful day,
When at last I reach the end of my journey,
Then the answer will surely come my way.

## Life's Worth

When I was just a lad,
So free from stress and strife,
There were those that loved me,
And taught me all about life.

I learned how to laugh,
And I learned how to cry,
I learned how to love,
But I never learned how to die.

When I grew much older,
Far away in a land war torn,
I witnessed pain and suffering,
And heard deaths quiet horn.

Upon my triumphant return,
To the land of my birth,
So many people told me,
My life had no worth.

And so I hung my head in shame,
But to the heavens silently I cried,
Till I heard a small voice within me,
Your worth is in your own eyes.

# Poems

Poems come from the heart,
Not from a silly book or the mind,
They should comfort the faint of heart,
And give sight to the spiritually blind.

Poems inspire others to be their best,
And bring out the best of all mankind,
Poems give all men a chance to rest,
So in their soul, peace they can find.

Poems don't have to ring or rhyme,
Just need to show the great flow of life,
Poems dig through life's deepest grime,
And help to respite life's toil and strife.

Poems are a person's deepest feelings,
Laid out in verse for all the world to see,
They can tell of a person's deepest desire,
So their hearts and minds can be open and free.

So sit and take your paper and pen,
And show the thoughts of your soul,
Show to all the women and men,
Life's wonderful, glorious goal.

## Freedom

I look out my window,
And what do I see,
People walking to and fro,
Thinking they are free.

Perhaps they do not see,
Or just don't understand,
True freedom can only be,
In the heart and the soul of a man.

Freedom is the right,
Of the great and small,
But for freedom, you must fight,
And answer the clarions call.

Vigilance is the only key,
That all people must keep,
To insure that all are free,
For this we must not sleep.

So keep the watch my friend,
By the day and by the night,
For we all must forever defend,
Freedom for all, for this is our right.

## My Wife

To my wife I must say,
For tomorrow, and today,
You are my life, my heart, my soul, my all.
With me you have stood,
Thru the bad and good,
And I know for all time our love will not fall.

Strength is what you give,
You always help me to live,
Through all of life's toils, cares, and strife.
I look upon your face now,
And renew my faithful vow,
For you are my life, my soul, my wife.

Worthy, I know I'll never be,
Of the love you give to me,
Happy and content, I will walk by your side.
We will let others see,
How true love can be,
When lovers walk with a vibrant stride.

I pledge my undying love,
To my wonderful dove,
And hope and pray side by side we will always be.
To you my heart I give,
And I know I will live,
A life that is content, as content as a man can be.

## My son

I look upon my son,
And think of all the fun,
We had when he was just a small carefree lad.
To manhood he has grown,
I guess I had always known,
That one day he would pull away from his dad.

I have taught him as he grew,
About the old and the new,
In hopes his path would be straight, true, and strong.
I see my cute little boy,
Put away his childhood toy,
Now to the world of manhood he will always belong.

No matter how big he grows,
Nor how far away he goes,
My little boy is what I'll always remember and see.
As he walks through this life,
Amid the struggles and strife,
A good and upright man I know he will always be.

Gone now is the little boy,
But not the wonder and the joy,
For my sweet little man he shall always be.
I hope to someday see,
The man he has come to be,
But in my heart it's the little boy I will see.

As through your busy life you run,
Be sure you stop and have some fun,
For they grow up faster than the eye can see.
These days will never again return,
Too late the lesson you will learn,
Your cute little boy, a man he will too soon be.

## My Daughter

She was cute and sweet,
Kind of nifty, kind of neat,
But into a beautiful woman she has grown.
But my little girl she will be,
Because I refuse to see,
The lady others now have loved and known.

Little freckles were on her face,
For me now there is no place,
In the life of the little girl I loved and helped to raise.
In my heart she will always stay,
For she has shown me the way,
How to live, love, and make the most of all my days.

Children of her own she has now,
And I sit back and think, wow,
My little girl has grown to a fine lady and mother.
I see her now, all grown,
In my heart I quietly mourn,
My loving daughter loves and clings to another.

In my heart I will always see,
The little girl God gave to me,
To nurture and teach the ways of love and life.
To the world she now belongs,
My heart sings sad and happy songs,
For now she has become a mother and a wife.

They say now my job is done,
But it seemed it had just begun,
In teaching and protecting her in a world of strife.
No need for me she has now,
The gray haired man with a scowl,
For now she walks her own path through this life.

## Stars

I look up into the vast black of night,
When other people slumber and sleep,
I see the myriad of stars shining bright,
Wonder and awe into my soul does creep

So close they seem that I could touch them,
Shining so brightly on a canvas of black,
Each looking like an exquisite precious gem,
They seem to be watching and looking back.

I know they are really suns like our own,
With other planets spinning round about,
For many years man's path they have shown,
Without them, lost would be man without a doubt.

But still it is the great wonder I tend see,
Watching the stars hung high in the sky,
Wishing in my heart that one day I could be,
As shining a beacon, flying so very high.

Perhaps one day our people will travel,
To many of those bright points of light,
Many mysteries to explore and unravel,
To live among those stars shining so bright.

But when that great day has finally come,
When mankind has visited those wonderful stars,
Will we forget the wonder and become numb,
To the beauty and spender that once was ours.

I hope mankind will always be able to see,
The beauty and wonder of the sky at night,
It is my prayer, my hope, my eternal plea,
We always see the stars, with wonder and delight.

# Love can be Pain

Love can sometimes bring pain,
So it looks like there is no gain,
In loving someone with all your heart and soul.
But with the pain, joy can be found,
And happiness in life can abound,
Love can make a broken heart become whole.

True love is the driving force,
It helps a person stay the course,
Through all of life's toils, cares, and woes.
Without love, life never can be,
Peaceful, hopeful, serene, or free,
For it is love that gives life its' perfect repose.

True love can take many forms,
It can weather all of life's storms,
It is love that makes a life worth the living.
Love can make a dark day bright,
It can make the heavy burden lite,
Love is what gives life its' only true meaning.

Seek the love your heart does crave,
A happier path through life you will pave,
It will give your life joy, comfort, and lasting peace.
Lovers that are walking side by side,
Will walk through life with easy stride,
Together, all of life's troubles will begin to cease.

Treat your partner with loving care,
Your whole heart you must share,
Hold tightly together through the storms of life.
Life's worst rapids you can still,
Your heart's desire you can fill,
For together, you will overcome worries and strife.

# Babbling Brook

I see the babbling brook,
Winding along its' merry way,
I wonder as I begin to look,
How peaceful it seems to sway.

It seems to flow so easily,
No worries or cares to show,
It just flows along so peacefully,
With serenity I wish I could know.

Life seems to flow so very fast,
With very little time to rest,
Before we know it, our time is past,
Never giving life our very best.

We need to slow our lives down,
Perhaps to count each and every tree,
If not, it is very likely we will drown,
In the furious pace life seems to be.

A wise and wonderful lesson we can learn,
From that babbling brook flowing so easily,
As the worries and woes of life we burn,
It is then we will learn to live so peacefully.

I saw a peaceful babbling brook,
Winding along its' merry way,
Understanding as I began to look,
How life can have that peaceful sway.

# The Spirit of Man

The Spirit of Man can never decline,
The Spirit of Man will always shine,
Through the darkest night, and the brightest day.
The Spirit of Man can soar so high,
Through the heavens, beyond the sky,
For the Spirit of Man forever is here to stay.

The Spirit of Man will always grow,
The universe will soon come to know,
The greatness and goodness of the Spirit of Man.
Though eons will continue to pass,
Mankind will continue to surpass,
Every single expectation, hope, plot, and plan.

Though the spirit may sometimes gray,
There will always come that bright day,
When the spirit will glow with light once again.
For the Spirit of Man will always find,
True greatness though peace of mind,
In this world the Spirit of Man will always reign.

One day my death will come,
No matter how far I try to run,
One day to its end, my journey will surely come.
But I know Spirit of Man will always be,
A shining beacon for the universe to see,
For to death, The Spirit of Man will never succumb.

In the next life, I will certainly know,
The Spirit of Man will continue to grow,
To light the way for all creatures great and small.
I know long after I am gone,
The Spirit of Man will live on,
For the Spirit of Man I know will never stall.

# The Clown

We see the silly funny clown,
Sometimes a smile, sometimes a frown,
He brings great laughter to the young and old.
He wears odd and funny cloths,
He sometimes has a really big nose,
He can warm the heart that has grown cold.

Beneath the bright colored paint,
You will never find a saint,
But a man no different than you, or even me.
To the crowd he is as funny as can be,
In private, simply an ordinary man is he,
Behind the curtain, where no one else can see.

He will make you laugh out loud,
Whether in your home, or in a crowd,
His antics are the strangest you'll ever see.
His gestures are big and vast,
The laughter seems to last,
Living sometimes longer than the oldest tree.

Then he goes to another town,
With his great smile and his frown,
To entertain more children of every kind and age.
He'll put on his wonderful show,
Very few will ever really know,
The man behind the paint when he leaves the stage.

I love to think of the funny clown,
When I'm lonely, or when I'm down,
The memory will always bring a smile to my face.
The clown is what I really want to see,
Acting as silly and funny as I want to be,
In my heart, he lives forever in a very special place.

When again a clown you chance to meet,
In the great big circus, or just on the street,
Greet him with a hand shake and a great big smile.
To a clown, laughter is the greatest joy,
From the strongest man, or the smallest boy,
It's the laughter that makes his life worthwhile.

But as you begin to walk away,
In your heart don't forget to say,
My life is so much better, for today I met a clown.
Then when you begin to fall asleep,
Count funny clowns, instead of sheep,
You'll wake with a big smile, instead of a frown.

## Life is a Play

Life is a play,
Or so they say,
And all the world a stage.
But this play is very sad,
And it makes me very mad,
To see people locked in a cage.

So get the key,
And set me free,
From all my worries and woes.
For it is in death,
And my last breath,
My soul shall fly and grow.

## Fate of Man

Is there an ultimate plan,
For the fate of every man,
If so, then what is the ultimate plan for me?
Will fate allow us to know,
How our plan is meant to grow,
Or are we to walk blindly into the sea?

If man's fate is truly his own,
Then why can't it be known,
What path through this life is best to use?
So many paths there are,
Going on so wide and so far,
How can we know which path to choose?

I really would like to know,
If I should run fast or slow,
For I cannot see beyond the next tree,
Show me the path that's best,
Then I know I'll past the test,
For an upright man is what I want to be.

As through this life we walk,
Let us take very careful stock,
With all that life's plan has for us to be.
Then we can begin to know,
How to help the plan to grow,
Then we can be all we are meant to be.

## Men and Women

Men and Women are the same,
When you look beneath the frame,
Into the heart, the spirit, the soul, the mind.
Beneath the surface you will see,
How great everyone can truly be,
Don't allow their gender to make you blind.

Treat everyone the same as you,
Would want to be treated too,
Only then the truth you'll be able to know.
Treat everyone with respect,
Your prejudice you must check,
Then you'll see how peaceful life can flow.

Women can be soft, nice, and sweet,
There is no challenge they can't meet,
Their inner strength they sometimes hide.
On the surface men can seem hard,
Many men put up a constant guard,
So others cannot see their gentler, softer side.

Battle of the Sexes is how it's known,
Out of proportion it seems to have blown,
For we are all together and on the same side.
Treating each other with loving respect,
This is how we can begin to perfect,
The human condition and span this tide.

So my friends let us move on,
Past the darkness into the dawn,
So all can continue to flourish and grow.
Brothers and sisters is what we are,
Working together we'll go so far,
Only then will life obtain that peaceful flow.

## Miracles

A miracle you want to see,
Then look at a baby or a tree,
Miracles you can see everywhere you look.
Miracles can be big or small,
On God you don't have to call,
They are found in every cranny and nook.

Look inside the human heart,
It is there you will find your start,
In your search for the miracles you seek.
Then look into the blue sky,
As the clouds go floating by,
Miracles happen every day of every week.

Watch a new life as it is born,
Even skeptics cannot scorn,
The miracle this new born life represents.
Every single face is unique,
From the proud to the meek,
These are some of the miracles life presents.

Look in your own backyard,
You don't have to look very hard,
Just open your eyes and miracles you'll see.
See life's greatest surprise,
Look at a sunset or a sunrise,
Nature gives you these wonders for free.

The next time you see a star,
Or even something really bizarre,
They are nature's gift given to me and you.
Look around and see nature's gift,
Your mind and soul will get a lift,
Nature's own recipe for her Miracle Brew.

# Teachers

Teaching is the biggest key,
To keep our country strong,
Teaching our children how to be free,
Teaching them right from wrong.

Mighty soldiers the teachers are,
Fighting ignorance and apathy,
On their door there should be a star,
For they are our greatest cavalry.

Teachers have earned our respect,
They light our path along the way,
In molding minds they are adept,
Never allowing good minds to stray.

For granted they are sometimes taken,
Sometimes we forget how hard they work,
It seems sometimes they have been forsaken,
Their contributions we sometimes shirk.

The love of their life teaching can be,
Educating all that are willing to learn,
Allowing the mind to be open and free,
This is the desire within them does burn.

I wish to honor those men and women,
For hearts and minds they open for all,
From rooftops, I'll shout it again and again,
You are the best, so stand proud and tall.

## A Man

Outside a man can be a real pig,
Sometimes you really have to dig,
To find the real man hiding deep inside.
The man inside can be very sweet,
His softer side can be very discrete,
But when he is loved his heart opens wide.

Find the man hidden deep inside,
Then like Dr. Jekyll and Mr. Hide,
The real good inside man you will reveal.
Treat him with tender loving care,
All your love with him you share,
You will have a real man, good and genteel.

Take his heart into your hand,
Watch that small heart expand,
It takes loving care to open up his heart.
Your just rewards will be great,
When you make him your mate,
From you, he will never be able to part

When you walk with him side by side,
Walking together with an even stride,
A path for the two of you the world will make.
Once you found him, never let him go,
You'll be amazed how far he can grow,
Patience and lots of love is what it will take.

Yes, a man can really be a pig,
But if you are willing to dig,
You'll find a loving faithful man inside.
You'll find he can be very sweet,
But you'll need to be very discrete,
Then to you, his heart will open very wide.

# Friendship

What is a true friend,
When does it begin,
When you trust someone more than any other?
Your friends you wisely choose,
You hope you don't lose,
For when that trust is broken then both suffer.

For a lifetime a true friend should be,
True friendship that's open and free,
Faith and hope will fill your heart and soul.
Treat this friend with loving care,
Someone, with whom you can share,
Your deepest secrets and your lifetime goal.

Look for friends where you live,
Where both can take and give,
Never breaking the trust that has been given.
The vital key is keeping trust,
For true friendship, this is a must,
For trust is how friendships must be driven.

True friends always forgive,
Even when you fail to live,
To the fullness of life you both know you can.
True friends will never judge,
They never carry any grudge,
But are always your biggest and loudest fan.

A friend for life everyone should find,
Someone, with whom you can unwind,
Someone to share your mind, your soul, your heart.
A true friend is the greatest treasure,
It will bring you the greatest pleasure,
A lifetime of hope and joy, a true friend will impart.

# My Doggie

I love my sweet doggie,
Sometimes she acts foggy,
She runs looking for something to bark at.
This dog runs so very fast,
I can't see how she can last,
At times, I think she is just a real dingbat.

She seems so very sweet,
When she sits at my feet,
Without reserve, her love she will freely give.
Her bark can be very loud,
I think because she is proud,
Telling the world this is how dogs should live.

When very excited she gets,
She runs around in a blitz,
Like a raging bull, many things get moved.
A big dog with a puppy's heart,
Back and forth she'll quickly dart,
Not understanding why we don't approve.

She can eat us out of house and home,
Food she guards like a greedy gnome,
She acts as though this food is the last she'll get.
Constantly, she can lick your hand,
Your full attention she will demand,
You must give in because she will never quit.

But she's become part of our family,
Without her, life would be real agony,
We have really grown to love her cute face.
We think our doggy is really great,
To us at the very top she does rate,
For we know our doggie we can never replace.

## A Soldier's Toast

On January 1, 1972, at 12:05 AM, I was asked to give a toast at a New Year's Eve Party while serving at the 24th Evac. Hospital in Long Bien, Vietnam. I have presented this toast every year at 12:05 AM to commemorate that night. I included it here in the hopes that all my readers will join me every January 1st at 12:05 AM in raising a glass to peace. General McArthur once said, **"The soldier, above all other people, prays for peace, for he must suffer and bear the deepest wounds and scars of war."** I completely agree with the General, so join me if you will:

To old soldiers, may they become extinct,
Extinct because there are no more wars,
No more wars because there truly is
PEACE ON EARTH!

TO PEACE, MY FRIENDS, TO PEACE!

# That Was My Mother

(A TRUE STORY OF A MOTHER'S HEART)

When my orders to go to Vietnam came, I was serving as a medic at the U.S. Army Hospital emergency room at Fort Polk in Louisiana, working the grave yard shift. I decided to call my mother in Indiana, trying to soften the blow, telling her I'd be home on a thirty day leave, but then I'd be going to Vietnam. I was soon to discover this was a big mistake.

Shortly after my call to my mother, I received notice to report to the company commander's office after my duty shift ended. As soon as my shift was over, I reported to the Captain's office, this is what transpired:

"Private Gray reporting as ordered, sir"

"Gray sit you're ass down," the captain gruffly replied.

Sitting down, I wondered what it was I did to make the captain so angry.

"Gray, why am I getting a call from the Commanding General at Fort Benjamin Harrison?" the Captain inquired.

"I haven't the foggiest idea, sir" I said very confused.

"Well, he wants you in my office when he calls," the Captain informed me.

At this point, my confusion was at its' ultimate high. As a private, I had no reason to have any dealings with a General. The phone rang before I could contemplate why a General would be interested in a lowly Private.

"Yes sir," the Captain answered, then again "Yes sir," he paused, "He is sitting right here sir."

Then handing the phone to me, he said, "He wants to talk to you."

Taking the phone trembling, I said with a shaky voice, "Yes sir, this is Private Gray."

"Gray, why did I get a call from your mother wanting to know why I am sending you to Vietnam, have you kill people, then bring home and try you for murder?" The General's voice was not harsh, but more like that of a father's concern. You see this happened shortly after Lieutenant Calley was tried and convicted of the slaughter at My Lai.

My mother had called and complained to a Two Star General for sending her son to Vietnam. A TWO STAR GENERAL! She couldn't stop at a Captain, a Major, or a Colonel; she had to go all the way to a Two Star General.

Finally, I was able to stammer out, "First General, I want to apologize…"

"Don't you dare apologize for your mother," the General ordered. "I'm not calling to chew you out son; I am calling because I want to talk to a man whose mother cares enough to do something. But I am giving you a direct order, don't ever apologize for your mother again, do I make myself clear, Private?"

"Yes sir," was all I could manage to stammer.

I briefly spoke with the General, then after the Captain ended the call, he said, "Gray, you must be the luckiest or the unluckiest Medic in the entire Army. Now get out of my office and go to bed."

Again, the only thing I could say was, "Yes Sir."

By the time I got up from bed, the story of the phone call had traveled throughout the entire hospital. It was over a week before I could leave, one of the worst weeks of my life. People would stop me in the halls asking about the phone call with comments like, "Hey Gray, who is your mother going to call next, Nixon?" To which I would reply, "I wouldn't be surprised." I couldn't wait to leave Fort Polk, even if it meant I would be going to Vietnam. Serving in Vietnam sounded like a vacation compared to staying there with the humiliation of that call. After that, I didn't think I'd be surprised by anything my mother did, or that she could embarrass me more than she had already done. I was soon to discover I was absolutely and positively WRONG.

After going home on leave, and bawling out my mother about calling Generals, I reported to Fort Lewis, Washington to embark for Vietnam. The night before I departed, I called my mother to let her know I would be leaving the next day; I would write once I had arrived at my duty station, and I could give her an address where she could write back.

It took over three weeks for me to finally arrive at my duty station with the $7^{th}$ Battalion, $15^{th}$ Field Artillery; after a few more days, I was assigned to a Battery. I reported to the Battery Commander on a Friday afternoon. The Captain informed me he had to go to the rear for a meeting but would be back the next day and we could get better acquainted. He told me in the meantime to get myself squared away and get to know the officers and men.

The next day, the Captain returned, and seeing me, yelled, "Doc, get your ass over here, NOW." You have to understand, our Captain had a voice so loud he could give an order in Vietnam, and you'd hear it back in Indiana.

I ran to the Captain's jeep, "Yes Sir."

"Doc, get your ass in my hooch, now," he ordered in an annoyed voice.

As I entered his hooch, I couldn't think of what I had done to annoy the Captain. I had been with the unit for less than a day; I was positive that I couldn't be in trouble already.

"Doc, I just had my ass chewed out by the Battalion Commander, that had his ass chewed out by the Brigade Commander, that got a call from II Corp, that got a call from the Oakland Base Commander, that got a call from the Commanding General of Fort Harrison, wanting to know why you haven't written your mother," the Captain said with one long sentence.

"Captain, I have been moving around and just got here…" I tried to explain.

"Doc" the Captain interrupted, "I don't want to hear it. Here's a pen, here is some paper, write your mother now. I'll personally put it in the mail, and I don't want to hear about this matter again, DO I MAKE MYSELF CLEAR, PRIVATE?"

"Yes sir," I meekly replied.

I wrote my mother and at the end, I placed a PS, "Mom, please quit calling Generals, they have more important things to do."

### THAT WAS MY MOTHER!

## About the author:

Phillip Gray served in the Army Medical Corp for over 6 years. While serving as a Combat Medic in Vietnam he was awarded the Purple Heart, the Combat Medical Badge, the Bronze Star, and the Silver Star. At the age of 50 he finally graduated from Indiana University/Purdue University at Indianapolis with a Bachelorette Degree in General Studies. Phillip also does amateur (open mike) stand-up comedy in the area around Indianapolis, Indiana and enjoys bartending. He hails from central Indiana where he currently lives with his wife of 16 years.

Made in the USA
Middletown, DE
11 August 2015